Macroeconomics for Managers

Roggie Clark

Avoid Credit Card Debt With This Book

Are you tired of living paycheck to paycheck? Drowning in interest rates and minimum payments that never seem to shrink your balance? *Understanding & Overcoming Credit Card Debt* is your roadmap to financial freedom.

https://www.amazon.com/dp/B0F3WCVWG8

Avoid Wasting Money On Crypto With This Book

Whether you're curious, cautious, or ready to invest, this book breaks down complex topics into plain language and cuts through the noise, buzzwords, and get-rich-quick schemes.

https://www.amazon.com/Think-Before-You-Crypto-Understanding-ebook/dp/B0F3YQ1L2Q

Learn How To Invest in Gold Bars With This Book

Whether you're new to investing or seeking to diversify your portfolio, this beginner-friendly guide will give you the knowledge and confidence to invest in gold, and other precious metals.

https://www.amazon.com/Ultimate-Investing-Buying-Guide-Beginners-ebook/dp/B0F1KWWDXG

Learn How To Invest in Silver With This Book

Whether you're approaching retirement or already enjoying it, protecting and growing your wealth is critical. The Ultimate Silver Investing & Buying Guide For Beginners is your clear, no-nonsense guide to incorporating silver into your wealth-building strategy.

https://www.amazon.com/Ultimate-Silver-Investing-Buying-Beginners-ebook

Copyright

Title: Macroeconomics for Managers
Author: Roggie Clark

Disclaimer

The views and opinions expressed in this book are those of the author and do not necessarily reflect the official policy or position of any individual, company, or organization cited or referenced in the text. The author is not affiliated with any of the individuals, companies, or organizations mentioned in the text, nor does the author receive any form of compensation for citing or referencing them.

The professional information in this text is distributed on an "as is" basis, without warranty. While every precaution has been taken in the preparation of the text, neither the author nor the publisher shall have any liability to any person or entity with respect to any loss or damage caused or alleged to be caused directly or indirectly by the instructions contained in this text or by the computer software and hardware products described in it.

The author nor the publisher does not guarantee any specific results or outcomes, and the information provided in this text should not be construed as professional advice. Readers should always consult with a qualified professional before making any significant changes to their website or business.

By reading this text, you agree that the author nor the publisher is responsible for any direct, indirect, incidental, or consequential damages that may arise from the use of the information provided. You assume full responsibility for any actions taken based on the information presented in this text.

Table of Contents

Introduction

Macroeconomics is often talked about in headlines, reports, and forecasts, but rarely explained in a way that feels useful for everyday business decisions. Terms like inflation, interest rates, and economic growth are constantly mentioned, yet many managers struggle to connect these ideas to what actually happens inside their business. The reality is that macroeconomics is not distant or abstract, it directly shapes the environment you operate in. Every pricing decision, hiring decision, and strategic move you make is influenced by broader economic forces, whether you recognize it or not.

Why This Book Exists

The problem with most macroeconomics content is that it is either too theoretical or too disconnected from real-world application. It often focuses on explaining how the economy works in general, but not how those dynamics impact the day-to-day decisions managers must make.

This book was created to close that gap.

Instead of treating macroeconomics as something to study, this book treats it as something to use. The goal is to help you understand how large-scale economic forces influence your business and how you can respond in a way that improves your outcomes.

Managers do not need to become economists. They need to become better decision-makers.

Macroeconomics as a Decision-Making Tool

At its core, macroeconomics is about understanding the bigger picture.

It examines how the overall economy behaves, including factors like inflation, interest rates, unemployment, and economic cycles. These forces influence how customers spend, how businesses invest, and how markets evolve over time.

For managers, this means macroeconomics provides context.

It helps answer questions like:

- Why are customers spending less right now?
- Why are costs increasing across the board?
- Why is it harder or easier to hire talent?
- Why are borrowing and financing conditions changing?

Without this context, managers are often left reacting to changes without fully understanding why they are happening.

With it, they can anticipate trends and make more informed decisions.

What Makes This Book Different

This book is not designed to overwhelm you with complex models or technical explanations. It is designed to simplify macroeconomics into clear, practical insights that you can apply immediately.

Each concept is explained with a focus on how it impacts real business decisions. Instead of focusing on theory alone, the emphasis is on application.

You will learn how to interpret economic trends, understand what they mean for your business, and adjust your strategy accordingly.

This approach allows you to:

- Make better pricing and cost decisions
- Plan more effectively for growth or slowdown
- Manage risk in uncertain environments
- Respond strategically instead of reactively

The goal is clarity, not complexity.

Who This Book Is For

This book is designed for managers, business owners, team leaders, and professionals who want to better understand the economy without getting lost in academic theory.

It is especially useful if you:

- Make strategic or financial decisions
- Manage budgets, pricing, or operations
- Need to plan for uncertain economic conditions
- Want to understand how economic trends affect your business

You do not need a background in economics to benefit from this book. You only need a willingness to think more intentionally about how the economy influences your decisions.

How to Use This Book

You can read this book from beginning to end to build a structured understanding of macroeconomics, or you can focus on specific chapters based on your current challenges.

If you are dealing with rising costs, focus on inflation. If you are evaluating financing or investment decisions, focus on interest rates. If you are planning for future growth, focus on economic cycles.

As you read, focus on understanding rather than memorization.

The value of macroeconomics is not in knowing definitions, it is in applying insights. The more you connect these ideas to your own business experiences, the more useful they become.

The Bigger Picture

When you begin to understand macroeconomics, patterns start to emerge.

You begin to see why certain strategies work better in some environments than others. You start to recognize how external forces influence your internal decisions. Instead of reacting to economic changes, you begin to anticipate them.

This shift in perspective is powerful.

It allows you to operate with greater clarity and confidence, even in uncertain conditions.

Last Thoughts

Macroeconomics is not about predicting the future with certainty, it is about improving how you respond to change. As a manager, your role is not to control the economy, but to understand it well enough to make better decisions within it.

This book is your starting point.

As you move forward, focus on applying what you learn. Pay attention to how economic trends influence your business, and use that awareness to guide your decisions. The more you practice this approach, the more natural it becomes.

With that foundation in place, the next step is to develop the mindset needed to interpret the economy through a managerial lens and understand why macroeconomics truly matters for the decisions you make every day.

Chapter 1: Thinking Like a Manager in a Macroeconomic World

Macroeconomics is often presented as something that happens "out there" in the broader economy, separate from day-to-day business decisions. In reality, it is deeply connected to everything managers do. Changes in inflation, interest rates, employment, and economic growth all influence how businesses operate. The challenge is not just understanding these concepts, but learning how to interpret them in a way that supports better decision-making. This chapter focuses on developing a managerial way of thinking about the economy, one that turns macroeconomic information into practical insight.

Why Macroeconomics Matters for Managers

Managers make decisions within an economic environment that is constantly changing. Even if you are focused on internal operations, external economic forces are always at play.

For example:

- Rising inflation can increase costs and reduce customer purchasing power
- Changes in interest rates can affect borrowing and investment decisions
- Economic growth or slowdown can influence demand for your products or services

Ignoring these factors does not eliminate their impact. It only makes decisions less informed.

Macroeconomics matters because it helps managers understand the forces shaping their business environment. Instead of reacting to changes after they happen, managers can begin to anticipate and prepare for them.

This leads to more strategic and less reactive decision-making.

The Difference Between Economic News and Real Impact

Economic information is everywhere. News headlines constantly highlight inflation rates, job reports, and central bank decisions. However, not all economic information is equally relevant to your business.

Managers must learn to separate noise from meaningful insight.

For example, a headline about rising inflation may sound important, but what matters is how that inflation affects your specific costs, pricing, and customer behavior. Similarly, a change in interest rates may be more or less relevant depending on your level of debt or reliance on financing.

The key is interpretation.

Managers should ask:

- How does this economic change affect my customers?
- How does it impact my costs and operations?

- What does this mean for my short-term and long-term strategy?

By focusing on impact rather than headlines, managers can make more relevant and informed decisions.

How the Economy Shapes Business Decisions

Macroeconomic forces influence nearly every area of a business.

Demand is affected by overall economic conditions. In a strong economy, customers may spend more freely. In a weaker economy, they may become more cautious.

Costs are influenced by factors like inflation and supply chain conditions. Rising costs may require adjustments in pricing or operations.

Access to capital is affected by interest rates and financial conditions. When borrowing becomes more expensive, businesses may delay expansion or reduce investment.

Hiring decisions are influenced by the labor market. In a tight labor market, it may be more difficult and costly to find employees.

These examples show that macroeconomics is not separate from business decisions, it is embedded within them.

Managers who understand this connection can make more informed and proactive choices.

Common Misunderstandings About the Economy

Many managers misunderstand macroeconomics because it is often presented in a simplified or abstract way.

One common misunderstanding is believing that economic trends affect all businesses equally. In reality, the impact can vary significantly depending on the industry, location, and business model.

Another misunderstanding is assuming that economic indicators provide clear and immediate answers. While indicators offer useful information, they do not guarantee specific outcomes. Managers must interpret them within the context of their own business.

There is also a tendency to overreact to short-term changes. Economic data can fluctuate, and not every change requires immediate action. Making decisions based on temporary shifts can lead to unnecessary adjustments.

Managers must develop a balanced perspective, recognizing both the importance and the limitations of economic information.

Building a Macroeconomic Mindset

Developing a macroeconomic mindset involves changing how you approach information and decisions.

Instead of viewing economic trends as background noise, you begin to see them as signals.

This mindset includes:

- Paying attention to key economic indicators
- Understanding how those indicators affect your business
- Thinking ahead rather than reacting after the fact
- Evaluating how external conditions influence internal decisions

It also involves accepting uncertainty.

Macroeconomics does not provide perfect predictions. Instead, it offers a framework for understanding possible outcomes and preparing for different scenarios.

Managers who adopt this mindset become more adaptable. They are better equipped to navigate changes and make decisions with greater confidence.

Last Thoughts

Thinking like a manager in a macroeconomic world means connecting what is happening in the broader economy to the decisions you make every day. It is about moving beyond headlines and focusing on real impact.

As you continue through this book, keep in mind that the goal is not to predict the economy perfectly, but to understand it well enough to make better decisions within it.

By developing a macroeconomic mindset, you create a foundation for interpreting trends, managing uncertainty, and responding strategically to change.

With this foundation in place, the next step is to understand economic growth and how it influences business expansion, demand, and opportunity.

Chapter 2: Economic Growth and Business Expansion

Economic growth is one of the most commonly discussed aspects of macroeconomics, yet it is often misunderstood by managers. It is typically presented as a single number or percentage, but behind that number are real changes in demand, opportunity, and business conditions. For managers, understanding economic growth is not about tracking statistics, it is about recognizing how expansion or slowdown affects decision-making. This chapter focuses on how economic growth influences business strategy and how managers can respond effectively.

What Economic Growth Really Means

Economic growth refers to the increase in the production of goods and services within an economy over time. While this definition is simple, its implications are significant.

Growth signals that:

- Businesses are producing more
- Consumers are spending more
- Overall economic activity is increasing

For managers, growth often translates into opportunity.

When the economy is expanding, customers may have more income, businesses may invest more, and demand for products and services tends to rise. This creates an environment where growth strategies, such as expanding operations or introducing new products, may be more successful.

However, growth is not uniform across all industries.

Some sectors may experience rapid expansion, while others grow more slowly or even decline. Managers must understand how broader economic growth relates specifically to their business.

GDP and Why It Matters for Business

Gross Domestic Product, or GDP, is the primary measure used to track economic growth. It represents the total value of all goods and services produced within an economy.

While GDP is often discussed in abstract terms, it has practical implications for managers.

When GDP is increasing:

- Demand is generally rising
- Business activity is expanding
- Opportunities for growth are more likely

When GDP is slowing or declining:

- Demand may weaken
- Businesses may become more cautious
- Competition for customers may increase

Managers do not need to focus on the exact calculation of GDP. Instead, they should understand what it signals about the overall direction of the economy.

GDP trends provide context for decision-making.

Growth vs Slowdown Environments

Economic conditions are not constant. Periods of growth are often followed by slowdowns or contractions. Each environment requires a different approach.

In a growth environment:

- Demand is typically stronger
- Businesses may expand operations
- Investment and hiring may increase

Managers may focus on capturing opportunities, scaling production, and increasing market share.

In a slowdown environment:

- Demand may weaken
- Customers may become more price-sensitive
- Businesses may reduce spending

Managers may need to focus on efficiency, cost control, and maintaining stability.

Recognizing which environment you are operating in is essential for making appropriate decisions.

How Growth Impacts Demand and Opportunity

Economic growth influences customer behavior.

When the economy is strong, customers are often more willing to spend. This can increase demand for both essential and non-essential products. Businesses may find it easier to attract customers and generate revenue.

During slower periods, customers may become more cautious. They may reduce spending, prioritize essentials, or seek lower-cost alternatives.

This shift in behavior directly affects demand.

Managers must adjust their strategies accordingly.

For example:

- In strong growth periods, businesses may invest in expansion or new offerings
- In slower periods, businesses may focus on retaining customers and optimizing pricing

Understanding how growth affects demand helps managers align their decisions with current conditions.

Planning During Expansion Periods

Periods of economic growth present opportunities, but they also require careful planning.

It can be tempting to expand quickly when demand is strong. However, overexpansion can create challenges if conditions change.

Managers should consider:

- Whether increased demand is sustainable
- How expansion will impact costs and capacity
- What risks may arise if growth slows

Strategic planning involves balancing opportunity with caution.

For example:

- Investing in scalable systems can support growth without overcommitting resources
- Maintaining financial flexibility can help manage future uncertainty
- Monitoring economic indicators can provide early signals of change

The goal is to take advantage of growth while remaining prepared for shifts in the economic environment.

Last Thoughts

Economic growth provides important signals about the direction of the business environment. For managers, the value lies not in the numbers themselves, but in understanding how those numbers translate into real opportunities and risks.

By recognizing the difference between growth and slowdown environments, and by adjusting strategies accordingly, managers can make more informed decisions and position their business for success.

Growth creates opportunity, but it also requires discipline. The most effective managers are those who can balance expansion with careful planning and long-term thinking.

With a clear understanding of economic growth, the next step is to explore inflation and how rising costs and changing purchasing power impact pricing, margins, and business strategy.

Chapter 3: Inflation and Pricing Strategy

Inflation is one of the most visible and impactful forces in the economy. It affects the cost of goods, the purchasing power of customers, and the overall financial health of businesses. For managers, inflation is not just a number reported in the news, it is something that directly influences pricing, costs, and strategy. Understanding how inflation works and how to respond to it is essential for maintaining profitability and staying competitive. This chapter focuses on how inflation shapes business decisions and how managers can adapt effectively.

What Inflation Is and Why It Happens

Inflation refers to the general increase in prices over time. As prices rise, the purchasing power of money decreases, meaning customers can buy less with the same amount of money.

Inflation can be caused by several factors.

One common cause is increased demand. When demand for goods and services grows faster than supply, prices tend to rise. Another cause is rising production costs. If businesses face higher costs for materials, labor, or transportation, they may pass those costs on to customers through higher prices.

External factors can also contribute, such as supply chain disruptions or changes in government policy.

For managers, the key takeaway is that inflation reflects changes in both demand and costs, and it affects how businesses operate at multiple levels.

How Inflation Affects Costs and Pricing

Inflation increases costs across the board.

Materials, labor, transportation, and operational expenses may all rise during inflationary periods. This creates pressure on margins, as businesses must decide whether to absorb these costs or pass them on to customers.

Pricing decisions become more complex.

If prices are increased too quickly, customers may reduce their demand. If prices are not increased at all, profit margins may shrink.

Managers must find a balance.

For example:

- Gradual price increases may help maintain demand while protecting margins
- Adjusting product sizes or offerings may help manage costs without significantly raising prices
- Improving efficiency can offset some cost increases

The goal is to maintain profitability while minimizing negative impacts on customer behavior.

Protecting Margins in Inflationary Periods

Margins are often most vulnerable during periods of inflation.

As costs rise, maintaining margins requires careful decision-making. Managers must evaluate where costs can be controlled and where pricing adjustments are necessary.

Some strategies include:

- Identifying and reducing unnecessary expenses
- Improving operational efficiency
- Renegotiating supplier agreements
- Adjusting pricing strategically

It is important to take a proactive approach.

Waiting too long to respond to rising costs can lead to significant margin compression. On the other hand, reacting too aggressively can harm customer relationships.

Managers must monitor costs closely and make adjustments based on both internal and external conditions.

Customer Behavior During Inflation

Inflation changes how customers behave.

As prices rise, customers may become more price-sensitive. They may look for lower-cost alternatives, reduce discretionary spending, or delay purchases.

However, not all products are affected equally.

Essential goods may continue to see stable demand, while non-essential items may experience a greater decline. Customer perception also plays a role. If customers believe price increases are justified, they may be more willing to accept them.

Managers must understand how their specific customer base responds to inflation.

This may involve:

- Monitoring changes in purchasing patterns
- Adjusting marketing and messaging
- Offering alternative pricing options or product variations

Understanding customer behavior allows managers to make more informed decisions.

Adjusting Strategy in Rising Cost Environments

Inflation requires managers to adapt their strategies.

This may involve:

- Reassessing pricing models
- Evaluating product offerings
- Adjusting cost structures
- Focusing on efficiency and value

Flexibility is essential.

Economic conditions can change quickly, and strategies that work in one environment may not work in another. Managers must be prepared to adjust as conditions evolve.

Long-term planning is also important.

While inflation presents challenges, it can also create opportunities for businesses that adapt effectively. Those who respond strategically can maintain stability and even gain a competitive advantage.

Last Thoughts

Inflation is a constant force that managers must navigate. It affects costs, pricing, and customer behavior, making it one of the most important macroeconomic factors to understand.

As a manager, your goal is not to eliminate the effects of inflation, but to respond to them effectively. By understanding how inflation impacts your business and adjusting your strategy accordingly, you can protect margins and maintain stability.

With a clear understanding of inflation, the next step is to explore interest rates and how they influence borrowing, investment, and overall business decision-making.

Chapter 4: Interest Rates and Business Decisions

Interest rates are one of the most influential forces in the economy, yet they are often misunderstood by managers. While they may seem like a financial detail reserved for banks or investors, interest rates affect how businesses borrow, invest, price, and grow. They influence customer behavior, access to capital, and overall economic activity. For managers, understanding interest rates is essential for making informed financial and strategic decisions. This chapter focuses on how interest rates work and how they impact real business outcomes.

What Interest Rates Represent

At a basic level, interest rates represent the cost of borrowing money and the return for lending it.

When interest rates are low, borrowing becomes cheaper. Businesses and consumers are more likely to take loans, invest, and spend. When interest rates are high, borrowing becomes more expensive, which can slow down spending and investment.

Interest rates are influenced by central banks and broader economic conditions.

Central banks often adjust interest rates to manage inflation and stabilize the economy. For example:

- If inflation is rising too quickly, interest rates may be increased to reduce spending

- If the economy is slowing down, interest rates may be lowered to encourage borrowing and investment

For managers, interest rates signal the overall financial environment.

They provide insight into whether conditions are more favorable for growth or caution.

How Rates Affect Borrowing and Investment

Interest rates directly impact borrowing decisions.

When rates are low:

- Loans are more affordable
- Businesses may invest in expansion, equipment, or new projects
- Consumers may increase spending

When rates are high:

- Loans become more expensive
- Businesses may delay or reduce investment
- Consumers may cut back on spending

Managers must consider how borrowing costs affect their decisions.

For example:

- Financing a new project may be more attractive when interest rates are low

- Paying off existing debt may become a priority when rates rise

Investment decisions should always account for the cost of capital.

Ignoring interest rates can lead to overinvestment during high-cost periods or missed opportunities during low-cost periods.

The Relationship Between Interest Rates and Demand

Interest rates also influence customer demand.

When borrowing is cheaper, customers may be more willing to spend, especially on larger purchases such as homes, vehicles, or high-value products. This can increase demand across various industries.

When borrowing becomes more expensive, customers may reduce spending, leading to lower demand.

This relationship affects businesses in different ways depending on their market.

For example:

- Businesses that rely on financing, such as real estate or automotive industries, may see significant changes in demand based on interest rates
- Businesses selling everyday goods may be less directly affected, but still experience changes in overall spending patterns

Managers must understand how interest rates influence their specific customer base.

Managing Debt and Financing Decisions

Debt is a common part of business operations, but it must be managed carefully.

Interest rates determine how expensive that debt becomes over time.

Managers should evaluate:

- The cost of existing debt
- The potential cost of new borrowing
- The impact of interest rate changes on future payments

For example:

- Variable-rate loans may become more expensive if interest rates rise
- Fixed-rate loans provide stability but may be less flexible

Understanding these differences helps managers make better financing decisions.

It is also important to consider risk.

Taking on too much debt during low interest rate periods can create challenges if rates increase later. Managers must balance opportunity with caution.

Strategic Planning in High vs Low Rate Environments

Interest rate environments influence overall business strategy.

In a low-rate environment:

- Expansion and investment may be more attractive
- Businesses may focus on growth opportunities
- Borrowing may be used to support scaling

In a high-rate environment:

- Cost control and efficiency become more important
- Businesses may prioritize stability over expansion
- Investment decisions may become more selective

Managers must adapt their strategies based on these conditions.

The goal is not to predict exact rate changes, but to understand how different environments affect decision-making.

By planning for both scenarios, managers can remain flexible and prepared.

Last Thoughts

Interest rates are a powerful force that shape how businesses operate. They influence borrowing, investment, customer demand, and overall economic activity.

As a manager, understanding interest rates allows you to make more informed decisions about financing, strategy, and risk. It helps you evaluate opportunities more clearly and avoid potential pitfalls.

The key is to view interest rates not as abstract numbers, but as signals that provide insight into the broader economic environment.

With this understanding, the next step is to explore unemployment and labor market dynamics, and how they influence hiring, wages, and operational decisions.

Chapter 5: Unemployment and Labor Market Dynamics

The labor market is one of the most important parts of the economy for managers. While metrics like inflation and interest rates often get more attention, employment conditions directly affect hiring, wages, productivity, and overall business operations. Understanding unemployment and labor market dynamics allows managers to make better decisions about staffing, compensation, and long-term planning. This chapter focuses on how the labor market works and how it impacts real business decisions.

What Unemployment Signals in the Economy

Unemployment measures the percentage of people who are actively looking for work but cannot find it. While this number may seem like a simple statistic, it provides valuable insight into the overall health of the economy.

Low unemployment generally signals:

- A strong economy
- High demand for labor
- Increased consumer spending

High unemployment often indicates:

- Economic slowdown
- Reduced business activity
- Lower consumer spending

For managers, unemployment is a signal of both opportunity and constraint.

A strong labor market can support higher demand for products and services, but it can also make it more difficult and expensive to hire employees. A weaker labor market may make hiring easier, but it may also signal reduced demand.

Understanding this balance is essential for making informed decisions.

Hiring, Wages, and Labor Availability

The availability of labor directly affects hiring decisions.

In a tight labor market, where unemployment is low, businesses compete for a limited pool of workers. This often leads to:

- Higher wages
- Increased competition for talent
- Greater emphasis on employee retention

In a loose labor market, where unemployment is higher, businesses may find it easier to hire workers. Wage pressures may decrease, and the pool of available candidates may increase.

Managers must adjust their approach based on these conditions.

For example:

- In a tight labor market, businesses may need to offer competitive compensation and benefits to attract talent

- In a looser market, businesses may have more flexibility in hiring and wage decisions

Understanding labor availability helps managers align their hiring strategies with economic conditions.

How Labor Markets Affect Business Costs

Labor is one of the largest costs for many businesses.

Changes in the labor market can significantly impact overall cost structures. Rising wages increase expenses, while lower wage pressure can help control costs.

However, focusing only on cost can be misleading.

Labor decisions also affect productivity, quality, and customer experience. Hiring lower-cost employees may reduce expenses in the short term, but it may also affect performance and long-term outcomes.

Managers must balance:

- Cost efficiency

- Employee quality

- Operational effectiveness

The goal is not simply to minimize labor costs, but to optimize them in a way that supports business performance.

Talent Competition and Retention

In competitive labor markets, attracting talent is only part of the challenge. Retaining employees becomes equally important.

High turnover can create:

- Increased hiring and training costs
- Disruptions in operations
- Loss of experience and knowledge

Managers must focus on creating an environment that encourages employees to stay.

This may include:

- Competitive compensation
- Opportunities for growth and development
- Positive workplace culture
- Clear communication and expectations

Retention strategies are especially important during periods of low unemployment, when employees have more options.

Understanding labor market conditions helps managers anticipate these challenges and respond proactively.

Adapting to Tight and Loose Labor Markets

Labor markets are not static. They change over time based on economic conditions.

Managers must be able to adapt.

In tight labor markets:

- Focus on retention and employee engagement
- Invest in training and development
- Consider automation or process improvements to reduce reliance on labor

In loose labor markets:

- Take advantage of increased labor availability
- Strengthen hiring processes
- Build a strong team for future growth

Flexibility is key.

By adjusting strategies based on labor market conditions, managers can maintain efficiency and position their business for success.

Last Thoughts

Unemployment and labor market dynamics provide important signals that influence hiring, wages, and overall business operations. For managers, understanding these signals is essential for making informed decisions.

The labor market is not just about numbers, it is about people. Effective management requires balancing cost, quality, and long-term strategy.

By understanding how labor markets function and adapting to changing conditions, managers can build stronger teams and more resilient businesses.

With a clear understanding of labor market dynamics, the next step is to explore economic cycles and how different phases of the economy influence business strategy and decision-making.

Chapter 6: Economic Cycles and Business Strategy

The economy does not move in a straight line. It expands, slows down, contracts, and recovers in patterns known as economic cycles. These cycles influence demand, costs, hiring, and overall business performance. For managers, understanding economic cycles is essential because strategies that work in one phase of the cycle may fail in another. This chapter focuses on how economic cycles work and how managers can adjust their strategies to align with changing conditions.

Understanding Economic Cycles

An economic cycle is the natural fluctuation of the economy over time. It typically consists of four phases:

- Expansion
- Peak
- Recession
- Recovery

During expansion, economic activity increases. Businesses grow, employment rises, and demand strengthens. At the peak, growth reaches its highest point before slowing down. A recession follows, characterized by declining economic activity, reduced demand, and increased uncertainty. Finally, recovery marks the period where the economy begins to improve and move back toward expansion.

These phases are not always predictable in timing or intensity, but they follow general patterns.

For managers, the goal is not to predict exactly when these phases will occur, but to recognize the signs and adjust accordingly.

Expansion, Peak, Recession, and Recovery

Each phase of the economic cycle creates different conditions for businesses.

In an expansion:

- Demand is generally strong
- Businesses invest and grow
- Hiring increases

Managers may focus on scaling operations, increasing production, and capturing market opportunities.

At the peak:

- Growth begins to slow
- Costs may rise due to increased demand
- Competition intensifies

Managers should begin to exercise caution, ensuring that growth is sustainable and not overextended.

During a recession:

- Demand declines

- Customers become more price-sensitive
- Businesses may reduce spending and hiring

Managers may need to focus on cost control, efficiency, and maintaining stability.

In recovery:

- Demand begins to increase again
- Business confidence improves
- Opportunities for growth re-emerge

Managers can gradually shift back toward expansion strategies while remaining cautious.

Understanding these phases helps managers align their decisions with current conditions.

How Cycles Affect Demand and Revenue

Economic cycles have a direct impact on demand.

During expansions, customers are more willing to spend, which can increase revenue across many industries. During recessions, spending often decreases, particularly for non-essential goods and services.

However, not all businesses are affected equally.

Some industries are more sensitive to economic cycles, while others remain relatively stable. For example:

- Luxury goods may see significant fluctuations in demand

- Essential goods may experience more consistent demand

Managers must understand how their specific business responds to economic cycles.

Revenue strategies should be adjusted accordingly.

For example:

- During strong periods, businesses may focus on growth and expansion
- During downturns, businesses may prioritize customer retention and cost management

Recognizing how cycles influence demand allows managers to plan more effectively.

Adjusting Strategy Across Different Phases

Effective managers adjust their strategies based on the phase of the economic cycle.

In expansion:

- Invest in growth opportunities
- Increase production and capacity
- Strengthen market position

At the peak:

- Monitor costs closely
- Avoid overexpansion

- Prepare for potential slowdown

During recession:

- Focus on efficiency and cost control
- Maintain cash flow
- Retain core customers

In recovery:

- Gradually reintroduce growth strategies
- Identify new opportunities
- Rebuild momentum

Adapting strategy helps businesses remain stable and competitive across different conditions.

Avoiding Reactive Decision-Making

One of the biggest mistakes managers make is reacting too quickly to short-term changes.

Economic cycles involve fluctuations, and not every change requires immediate action. Overreacting can lead to unnecessary adjustments that disrupt long-term strategy.

Managers should focus on:

- Identifying broader trends rather than short-term movements
- Making decisions based on patterns, not isolated data points

- Maintaining a long-term perspective

Balanced decision-making helps avoid instability.

Instead of reacting impulsively, managers should use economic cycles as a guide for strategic planning.

Last Thoughts

Economic cycles are a natural part of the business environment. They create both challenges and opportunities, depending on how managers respond.

By understanding the different phases of the cycle and adjusting strategies accordingly, managers can make more informed decisions and navigate changes with greater confidence.

The key is not to predict the exact timing of each phase, but to recognize patterns and remain flexible.

With a clear understanding of economic cycles, the next step is to explore how government policy influences the economy and how those changes impact business decisions.

Chapter 7: Government Policy and Business Impact

Government policy plays a significant role in shaping the economic environment businesses operate in. Decisions made by governments and central banks influence taxes, spending, borrowing costs, and overall market conditions. For managers, understanding these policies is essential because they affect costs, demand, and strategic planning. This chapter focuses on how government actions influence the economy and how managers can interpret and respond to those changes.

Fiscal Policy and Government Spending

Fiscal policy refers to government decisions about spending and taxation.

When governments increase spending, they inject money into the economy. This can stimulate demand, support businesses, and create jobs. For example, infrastructure projects or public programs can increase economic activity and create opportunities for businesses that supply goods or services.

When governments reduce spending or increase taxes, the opposite effect may occur. Demand can slow, and businesses may face reduced opportunities.

Managers should pay attention to fiscal policy because it affects:

- Customer spending power
- Demand for products and services

- Overall business conditions

Understanding these effects helps managers anticipate changes in the market.

Monetary Policy and Central Banks

Monetary policy is managed by central banks and focuses on controlling the money supply and interest rates.

Central banks adjust interest rates to manage inflation and economic stability. For example:

- Lowering interest rates can encourage borrowing and spending
- Raising interest rates can reduce inflation by slowing demand

Monetary policy directly influences:

- Borrowing costs
- Investment decisions
- Consumer spending

Managers must understand how these changes affect their business.

For example:

- Lower interest rates may create opportunities for expansion
- Higher rates may require a more cautious approach

Monitoring central bank actions helps managers anticipate shifts in the economic environment.

Taxes, Regulations, and Business Decisions

Government policies also include taxes and regulations, which directly impact how businesses operate.

Changes in taxes can affect:

- Profitability
- Pricing decisions
- Investment strategies

For example:

- Higher taxes may reduce available profit and limit expansion
- Lower taxes may increase resources available for growth

Regulations can influence how businesses structure their operations.

These may include:

- Industry-specific rules
- Labor laws
- Environmental standards

While regulations can create challenges, they can also create opportunities for businesses that adapt effectively.

Managers must stay informed about these changes and adjust their strategies accordingly.

Policy Changes and Market Reactions

Markets often react quickly to changes in government policy.

Announcements about interest rates, taxes, or regulations can influence:

- Investor behavior
- Business confidence
- Customer expectations

These reactions can create short-term volatility, but they can also signal longer-term trends.

Managers should focus on understanding the broader implications rather than reacting to immediate changes.

For example:

- A new policy may initially create uncertainty but lead to long-term growth opportunities
- A change in interest rates may affect demand gradually rather than immediately

Interpreting these signals helps managers make more informed decisions.

Navigating Uncertainty from Policy Shifts

Government policy can introduce uncertainty.

Changes may occur quickly, and their effects are not always predictable. Managers must be prepared to operate in this environment.

Key approaches include:

- Staying informed about policy developments
- Evaluating potential impacts on the business
- Maintaining flexibility in decision-making

Scenario planning can be useful.

By considering different possible outcomes, managers can prepare for a range of situations rather than relying on a single expectation.

This reduces risk and improves resilience.

Last Thoughts

Government policy is a powerful force that influences the economic environment in which businesses operate. Understanding fiscal policy, monetary policy, taxes, and regulations allows managers to better interpret changes and adjust their strategies.

As a manager, your goal is not to predict every policy decision, but to understand how those decisions may impact your business and to respond thoughtfully.

By staying informed and maintaining flexibility, you can navigate policy changes with greater confidence and make decisions that align with both current conditions and long-term goals.

With a clear understanding of government policy, the next step is to explore global economics and how international markets and events influence local business decisions.

Chapter 8: Global Economics and Market Influence

No business operates in isolation from the global economy. Even if your company serves a local market, global forces such as trade, supply chains, currency movements, and international events can influence your costs, pricing, and overall strategy. Managers who understand global economics are better equipped to anticipate disruptions, identify opportunities, and make more informed decisions. This chapter focuses on how global economic forces shape business outcomes and how managers can respond effectively.

How Global Markets Affect Local Business

Global markets influence local businesses more than many managers realize.

Products, materials, and services often come from different parts of the world. Changes in global supply and demand can affect availability, pricing, and delivery times, even for businesses that operate domestically.

For example:

- A disruption in a major manufacturing region can increase costs for imported goods
- Increased global demand for certain materials can raise prices locally
- Economic growth in other countries can create new opportunities for expansion

Managers must understand that local performance is often connected to global conditions.

Recognizing these connections allows for better planning and more informed decision-making.

Trade, Supply Chains, and Costs

Trade and supply chains are central to global economics.

Businesses rely on supply chains to obtain materials, manufacture products, and deliver goods to customers. These supply chains often span multiple countries, making them vulnerable to global disruptions.

Changes in trade policies, transportation costs, or geopolitical events can impact supply chains.

For example:

- Tariffs can increase the cost of imported goods
- Shipping delays can disrupt production schedules
- Changes in trade agreements can affect availability and pricing

Managers must consider how these factors influence their cost structures and operations.

Diversifying suppliers, improving inventory management, and building flexibility into operations can help reduce risk.

Currency and Exchange Rate Impacts

Currency values play a significant role in global business.

Exchange rates determine how much one currency is worth relative to another. Changes in exchange rates can affect the cost of imports and the competitiveness of exports.

For example:

- A stronger domestic currency may make imports cheaper but exports more expensive
- A weaker domestic currency may increase the cost of imports but make exports more competitive

Even businesses that do not directly engage in international trade can be affected.

Currency fluctuations can influence supplier costs, competitor pricing, and overall market conditions.

Managers must be aware of these dynamics when making pricing and sourcing decisions.

Global Events and Business Risk

Global events can have significant and sometimes unexpected impacts on businesses.

These events may include:

- Economic crises
- Political instability
- Natural disasters

- Pandemics

Such events can disrupt supply chains, shift demand, and create uncertainty in markets.

Managers must be prepared to respond.

This involves:

- Monitoring global developments
- Assessing potential risks
- Developing contingency plans

Businesses that are prepared for disruptions are more resilient and better able to adapt.

Adapting to an Interconnected Economy

The global economy is highly interconnected.

Changes in one part of the world can quickly affect others. Managers must adopt a broader perspective when evaluating decisions.

This includes:

- Understanding how global trends affect local markets
- Recognizing the importance of flexibility
- Being prepared to adjust strategies as conditions change

Adaptation is key.

Managers who remain aware of global influences and adjust their approach accordingly are more likely to succeed in a dynamic environment.

Last Thoughts

Global economics adds another layer of complexity to business decision-making, but it also provides valuable insight into the forces shaping the market.

By understanding how global markets, trade, currency, and events influence your business, you can make more informed decisions and better manage risk.

As a manager, your goal is not to control global forces, but to understand them well enough to respond effectively.

With a clear understanding of global economic influences, the final step is to bring all of these concepts together and apply macroeconomic thinking to real business decision-making.

Chapter 9: Making Better Business Decisions With Macroeconomics

Macroeconomics is most valuable when it moves from theory into action. Throughout this book, you have explored how economic growth, inflation, interest rates, labor markets, cycles, policy, and global forces shape the business environment. The real advantage comes from bringing these concepts together and using them to guide decisions. Managers are not dealing with isolated variables, they are making decisions in a system where everything is connected. This chapter focuses on how to apply macroeconomic thinking in a practical and consistent way.

Connecting Economic Indicators to Decisions

Economic indicators provide signals about what is happening in the broader economy. However, their value depends on how they are interpreted and applied.

Managers must connect indicators to real business outcomes.

For example:

- Rising inflation may signal increasing costs and the need to adjust pricing
- Higher interest rates may suggest more cautious investment and borrowing decisions
- Changes in unemployment may affect hiring strategies and wage expectations

The key is not just to observe these indicators, but to understand their implications.

Managers should ask:

- How does this affect my customers?
- How does this affect my costs?
- What changes should I consider in response?

By linking indicators to decisions, managers can move from awareness to action.

Anticipating Trends Instead of Reacting

One of the biggest advantages of macroeconomic thinking is the ability to anticipate change.

Managers who rely only on current conditions often find themselves reacting too late. By paying attention to economic trends, managers can prepare for what is likely to happen next.

For example:

- Early signs of rising inflation may allow for gradual pricing adjustments
- Shifts in interest rates may signal changes in investment strategy
- Changes in economic growth may indicate future demand patterns

Anticipation reduces risk.

It allows managers to make proactive decisions rather than reactive ones.

Decision-Making Frameworks for Managers

A structured approach helps managers apply macroeconomic thinking more effectively.

A simple framework includes:

1. Identify Relevant Economic Signals
   Focus on the indicators that are most relevant to your business, such as inflation, interest rates, or employment trends.

2. Assess Impact
   Determine how these signals affect demand, costs, and operations.

3. Evaluate Options
   Consider different strategies based on possible outcomes.

4. Take Action and Monitor
   Implement decisions and track results, adjusting as needed.

This framework helps managers stay focused and avoid being overwhelmed by complexity.

Managing Risk and Uncertainty

Macroeconomics involves uncertainty.

Economic conditions can change quickly, and not all outcomes are predictable. Managers must be comfortable making decisions without perfect information.

Risk management becomes essential.

This includes:

- Maintaining financial flexibility
- Avoiding overcommitment during uncertain periods
- Preparing for multiple scenarios

Diversification and adaptability can also reduce risk.

Managers who plan for different outcomes are better equipped to handle unexpected changes.

Applying Macroeconomics in Daily Operations

Macroeconomic thinking should not be limited to major strategic decisions. It should be part of daily operations.

This may include:

- Adjusting pricing based on cost trends
- Monitoring customer behavior in response to economic changes
- Evaluating hiring and investment decisions based on economic conditions
- Staying informed about relevant economic developments

Over time, this approach becomes part of how managers think.

Instead of reacting to changes, they begin to anticipate and adapt more effectively.

Last Thoughts

Making better business decisions with macroeconomics is about using a broader perspective to guide your actions. It is not about predicting the economy perfectly, but about understanding it well enough to respond with clarity and confidence.

As a manager, your ability to interpret economic signals and apply them to your decisions is a powerful advantage. It allows you to navigate uncertainty, manage risk, and identify opportunities.

The more consistently you apply this approach, the more effective your decision-making will become.

You now have the framework. The value comes from using it.

Closing

Macroeconomics is often seen as something distant, something discussed in reports, forecasts, and headlines. But as you have seen throughout this book, it is not separate from your day-to-day decisions. It shapes the environment you operate in, influences how your customers behave, and affects how your business performs. The real value of macroeconomics is not in understanding every detail, but in knowing how to use it to make better decisions.

Bringing It All Together

Every concept in this book connects back to how decisions are made.

Economic growth influences demand and opportunity. Inflation affects costs and pricing. Interest rates shape borrowing and investment. Labor markets determine hiring and wages. Economic cycles create shifts in strategy. Government policy and global forces add additional layers of complexity.

These are not isolated ideas. They work together.

Managers who understand these connections are better equipped to evaluate situations and respond effectively. Instead of viewing each change as a separate challenge, they can see the broader pattern and make more informed decisions.

This is where macroeconomic thinking becomes powerful.

The Power of Consistent Awareness

You do not need to track every economic indicator or predict every shift in the economy. What matters is consistent awareness.

Pay attention to the key signals that affect your business:

- Changes in inflation and costs
- Movements in interest rates
- Trends in employment and demand
- Shifts in economic cycles

Over time, this awareness helps you recognize patterns.

You begin to understand not just what is happening, but why it is happening and what it may mean for your business.

This awareness supports better planning and more confident decision-making.

Thinking Beyond the Present

One of the most important benefits of macroeconomic understanding is the ability to think beyond the present moment.

Managers who focus only on current conditions may miss what is coming next. Those who consider economic trends can prepare for change.

This does not mean predicting the future with certainty. It means being ready.

By considering different scenarios and understanding how economic forces interact, managers can build strategies that are more flexible and resilient.

This reduces the impact of unexpected changes and creates opportunities to act ahead of competitors.

Final Thoughts

Macroeconomics is not about having all the answers. It is about asking better questions and making more informed decisions.

As a manager, your role is to navigate an environment that is constantly changing. The more you understand the forces shaping that environment, the better equipped you are to lead, adapt, and succeed.

This book has provided you with a framework. The next step is to apply it.

Pay attention to the economy. Connect what you observe to your decisions. Adjust your strategies as conditions change.

The more you do this, the more natural it becomes.

You now have a broader perspective and a stronger foundation for decision-making. Use it.

Glossary

This glossary provides clear, practical definitions of key macroeconomic terms used throughout the book. The goal is not just to define these concepts, but to reinforce how they connect to real business decisions.

Macroeconomics

The study of the overall economy, including factors like inflation, economic growth, unemployment, and government policy. For managers, it provides context for decision-making.

Economic Growth

The increase in the production of goods and services in an economy over time. Growth often signals expanding demand and business opportunity.

Gross Domestic Product (GDP)

The total value of all goods and services produced within an economy. It is commonly used to measure economic growth and overall economic activity.

Inflation

The general rise in prices over time, which reduces the purchasing power of money. Inflation affects costs, pricing, and customer behavior.

Purchasing Power

The amount of goods and services that can be bought with a given amount of money. As inflation increases, purchasing power decreases.

Interest Rates

The cost of borrowing money or the return on savings. Interest rates influence spending, investment, and overall economic activity.

Monetary Policy

Actions taken by central banks to control the money supply and interest rates in order to manage inflation and economic stability.

Fiscal Policy

Government decisions regarding spending and taxation that influence economic activity.

Unemployment

The percentage of people in the workforce who are actively seeking employment but cannot find a job. It reflects labor market conditions.

Labor Market

The supply of and demand for workers in an economy. It influences hiring, wages, and workforce availability.

Economic Cycle

The natural fluctuation of the economy over time, including expansion, peak, recession, and recovery phases.

Expansion

A phase of the economic cycle where economic activity is increasing, demand is strong, and businesses are growing.

Recession

A period of declining economic activity, reduced demand, and increased uncertainty.

Recovery

The phase following a recession where economic activity begins to improve.

Peak

The highest point of economic activity before a slowdown or recession begins.

Demand (Macroeconomic Context)

The overall level of spending in an economy. It is influenced by income, employment, and economic conditions.

Supply (Macroeconomic Context)

The total production of goods and services in an economy.

Aggregate Demand

The total demand for goods and services within an economy at a given time.

Aggregate Supply

The total supply of goods and services that businesses are willing to produce.

Exchange Rate

The value of one currency relative to another. Exchange rates affect the cost of imports and the competitiveness of exports.

Trade

The exchange of goods and services between countries. Trade influences supply chains, costs, and market opportunities.

Tariffs

Taxes imposed on imported goods, which can increase costs and affect pricing.

Central Bank

An institution responsible for managing a country's monetary policy, including setting interest rates and controlling money supply.

Economic Indicators

Data points that provide insight into the state of the economy, such as GDP, inflation rates, and unemployment levels.

Business Cycle Sensitivity

The degree to which a business is affected by changes in the economic cycle.

Risk

The possibility of loss or uncertainty in outcomes, often influenced by economic conditions.

Volatility

The degree of variation in economic or market conditions over time, often associated with uncertainty.

Last Thoughts

This glossary is meant to support your understanding, not replace it. These terms are most valuable when you see how they apply to real decisions.

As you continue to make decisions in your business or career, refer back to these concepts and consider how they influence your environment. Over time, they will become part of how you think, not just terms you recognize.

The more familiar you are with these ideas, the more confident and effective your decision-making will become.

About the Author

Roggie "Raj" Clark is an entrepreneur, author, and education minded creator whose work spans digital marketing, investing, economics, programming, and early academic development. With more than a decade of experience in ecommerce and digital business growth, he has built and managed successful online stores with thousands of sales and consulted for numerous marketing clients on branding, consumer behavior, and online strategy.

As a former marketing manager at a fintech company, Roggie gained firsthand experience in financial systems, wealth building strategy, and economic decision making. That experience inspired him to write books focused on investing, financial literacy, macro and microeconomics, and helping readers make informed long term financial decisions.

Roggie also holds a degree in Elementary Education and has a background in classroom teaching. Drawing from his academic training and educational experience, he has written classroom aligned books designed to support learning standards and structured skill development. His educational titles are intentionally crafted to blend clear instruction with engaging content that supports both classroom and homeschool learning environments.

Whether explaining search engine optimization, programming concepts such as HTML, CSS, and JavaScript, economic principles, or foundational academic skills, Roggie focuses on breaking complex topics into accessible learning experiences. Across every subject he writes about, his goal is to build strong foundations, encourage critical thinking, and equip readers with tools that support long term growth.

He lives in Maryland and continues to develop educational and business focused resources designed to inform, empower, and inspire.

www.ingramcontent.com/pod-product-compliance
Lightning Source LLC
LaVergne TN
LVHW022314200926
848481LV00004B/1334